FORTUNATE LIGHT

BY DAVID BERGMAN

D1797990

BODY LANGUAGE 09

A MIDSUMMER NIGHT'S PRESS

New York

Main cover photo *HotelShot Artisan* © 2009 by Ipedia1

A Midsummer Night's Press
16 West 36th Street
2nd Floor
New York, NY 10018
amidsummernightspress@gmail.com
www.amidsummernightspress.com

Designed by Aresográfico *www.diegoareso.com*

First edition, March 2013.

ISBN-13: 978-1-938334-02-3
ISBN-10: 1938334027

Printed in Spain.

CONTENTS

For Richard Howard

IN NORDSTROM'S

Anything could be written on this face—
he is that young and unmarked
by imperfection, the skin smooth, the green
eyes grass at dawn. He finds my toes
in the shoes that are too long. He brings
out a size smaller. "Walk on them," he says.
"How do they feel?" he asks. In the presence
of such beauty, one forgets one's age and then
grows painfully aware of it. "They look good
on you," he nods, smiling. And for the first time
I notice all his clothes are wrong,
that any clothing would be wrong on the fine
light structure of his bones that was built
only for wings. Just wings.

A VALENTINE

When we met we had only history
to bind us—the stories of those we'd known
before we knew each other—pale young men
and brawny ones, architects, and lawyers,
and we made love in the shadows of that
history like two shepherds sheltering
in the ruins of a Roman temple.

That was twenty years ago. Now there's so
much less history between us. Little
by little, we let it off like riders
on a bus pulling over to the curb,
the breaks hissing, the door clattering shut
as we watched the past left behind, clutching
its tattered briefcase or grocery bag.

Almost no one's left on board anymore,
just the old hag in the back who's snoring,
a sullen teen in twisted baseball cap,
a boy eating a sandwich his mother
wrapped for him, the companions we never
can be without and have no other place
to go to or call home. And we love them.

For the past has become just a method
of finding a way to face the present
and our futures: the one that is unknown
and the other that's inevitable.
For now our pockets are stuffed with tickets.
I lean back, rest my head on your shoulder,
and a wedge of geese split open the sky.

THE FORTUNATE LIGHT

How fortunate that starlight is kept
in the dark when setting out and does
not know how far it must go before

it has something to shine on. Lucky
the ray that finds a sliver of dust,
a cool moon close at hand though it must

glimmer there unseen. At least it will
never feel the cruel degradation
of violet's unavoidable shift

to red or become the unseen waves
of the radio, heard, if at all,
by the iron ears of radar

as it breaks on its revolving bars.
The beams of the black hole must be glad
to have found their home without leaving,

though it grows dense and incestuous
as a tenement. But happiest
of all must be this fortunate light

that tonight has, through open windows,
fallen on the closed lids of the one
who lies asleep and still beside me.

THE INFINITE RECESSION
OF THE OBJECT OF DESIRE

Although I haven't seen him in thirty years
or more, I dreamt last night of his passing
beneath me as I watched from a window,
closed against the chill of the early spring.

He is crossing a lawn that glows with green.
His back is to me, but I know it's him
from his walk, his body outlined with light
like the moon as it eclipses the sun,

circling him with a strand of liquid beads.
I've heard from friends' reports that he'd gone mad
or married, moved West to an ashram or
taken up the trumpet like his father.

It makes no difference. In my dream he is
just as he was. Only I am older
and I don't want him seeing me alone
in front of the window. What's strange is I

no longer crave him in my arms whereas
in college I lusted after him, frightening
myself with my desire. What does it mean

after more than thirty years that all I want

is that he stay framed between the mullions
of the window, held a little longer,
luminous and unaware that I am
watching him recede out of the picture?

THE BODY REMEMBERS

The body remembers what the mind forgets.
Actors know this, and when their parts require
long-forgotten rage, they make a fist
and anger arrives just as they desire.
Pianists, too, rely upon their hands
to recall a piece they haven't played for years
and marshal the keyboard under their command
before the music rises to their ears.
And lovers who have long remained apart
because of argument or circumstance,
will feel, before it builds up in their heart,
pressures along the arm, then their embrace
releases from lips an unexpected grace,
words that they'd forgotten how to start.

NARCISSUS

O said the lake
as he threw himself
into the still
body of water.

O said the lake
in surprise
and then pain
and finally in pleasure,

O after O
that radiated across
its never-before-troubled surface.

The water closed around him,
held him
(what did he know of swimming?)
and a few days later
let him float
bloated to the surface.

Love has ever since followed
the same circuitous pattern:

it starts in a plunge
and ends with a stink.

GANYMEDE

With that hot breath down my neck,
I knew at once: this is no bird.
But the gods like you to play along.

And I did. I kicked. And screamed.
Raised my hands against the hard
sleak beak lifting me up by my scruff.

Magnificient pecker. He didn't
start to molt into a man until
we landed well above the concerns

of mortals. It wasn't so strange.
Really. I knew from an early age
I was beautiful—engorgeous—

as my witty uncle used to say
as he dandled me on his knee.
The gods are only a bit less constrained.

Often I get groped as I serve them.
They like all their cups to runneth over,
And I've learned in time not to spill a drop.

THE EMBRACE

To hold you is not
to contain you much
less possess you—it
is a way to be
in contact with that
part of you that is
body and sense by
addition that part
of you that is not,
how even your breath
bears traces of life
that is more than air,
more than this heat, more
than the rasp of words.
I imagine I
can hear what may not
be words at all but
merely your presence
drawn across the flesh,
the self
abraded by what else
it is and must always be.

JOHN KOCH,
COCKTAIL PARTY, 1956

"This life disappeared with the Kochs"
–Roy Davis

If life might be rendered like a painting,
one could do worse than this: the late light
drawing the room into conversation,
lively, smart, the cocktails providing oil
to the hesitant tongue, though we're all friends
who need not worry about speaking our mind.

Anyway we're all of a similar mind,
alert to the nuances of music and painting
and the delicate feelings of our friends.
For every cigarette there'll be a light.
The lamp casts a sheen like virgin oil
on a red shawl backed in conversation

with the host who mirrors in conversation
his ample wife. She, for the moment, minds
the hors d'oevres that lie beneath the Vuillard oil
that has been invented for the painting.
In the left corner, out of direct light
an older man is talking to his "friend"

(No need to be vulgar, we know what "friend"
means in this sort of conversation),
not that their relationship is made light
of here, where we're far too worldly to mind,
and he has the youth and beauty a painting
calls for, his hair like honey or pressed oil,

though his lips blur as if this large oil
were still a work in progress. With friends
like these, you can't ever be done painting
or bring an end to the conversation.
There's always more to reveal of our mind,
some piquant development to bring to light.

Only the butler does not show delight
in his inclusion in this complex oil.
I can't help but think he's lost his mind,
the way he holds his arm against the friend,
seated below him in deep conversation,
as if protecting himself from the painting.

Well, he's no friend, the butler—black as oil—
but he hasn't blocked the light or conversation.
Pay no mind to what a servant thinks of painting.

THE MAN WHO WASN'T LOVED ENOUGH

He felt he wasn't loved enough.
Rain fell. Trees shook in the wind
like wet dogs. But what would be enough?

He did not know. He'd been loved
by a few, perhaps more than most.
It made no sense counting, or rather

the count meant nothing in the end.
What he had missed was a certain
intensity, something that would pierce

the membrane that covered the self
but through which the self
was always leaking. There was no face

behind the glass, only clouds injured
by jostling one another, and no lightning
which would've made it somehow

worth the bruises. Against the window,
the rain knocked, a liquid fist, wanting
not to be admitted, but to shatter.

PAIN TO FOLLOW

It must have been summer. It must have been hot.
I had not yet begun to go to school.
I was afflicted with the lethargy

that is the special disease of childhood:
sick of myself and angry that no one
knew what I did not know myself—what it was

I wanted. I had gone down to the basement
for what? To be alone? Because it was cool?
Because there I could stretch out on the tile

and do nothing? The floor was covered
with my toy cars, little match-box Chevys
and Fords in plastic, aluminum and lead.

There were twenty or so in red and green,
blue and banana yellow, yet none gleamed
as it had in its package. I bent my head

to imagine them racing down the highway
and instead I saw a vast junkyard. Chassis
gouged and smashed. One melted by a match,

axels twisted, doors cracked open,
re-cemented, and cracked again, paint-jobs
scratched and blistered. Not that I meant

to do harm. But I had, I had, and I knew
that I would do it again. For I saw clearly
no matter how kindly I treated my toys,

I could not save them from the destruction.
I had wrecked on them myself. This was my fate,
and nothing could change whatever I was.

Nearly sixty now I look across the waste
I have made. I touch the one whom most I love
and expect bruises, bleeding, pain to follow.

SCREWBALL COMEDY

He had not understood how much his life was ruled
by not knowing what he did not want to know,
but that was exactly what had to stay hidden.

Had he been sure of what he should not know,
he could have easily avoided it, just as he
had always kept himself vague about the balance

in his checkbook, his parents' anniversary, or the
               condition
of his upper molars, aware that being too up on these
               facts
would place on him obligations he did not wish to bear.

But to steer clear of knowing what you never
wanted to find out required a sensitive if unconscious
hand upon the tiller, a nearly empty ballast, and more

than usual luck, all of which he did not possess.
"I love you," his lover had told him quite casually,
as though it were the most obvious thing in the world,

"But I don't especially like you." And all at once
he knew the loneliness he felt and which he had tried

so long to deny was not a phantom of his imagination,

but a truth he would have to live with far longer
than his lover chose to stay with him. And he also knew
that he had never wanted to love or be loved–

feelings that always led to pain because of their
extremity. Instead he desired to be enjoyed
like a forties screwball comedy, something

with Myrna Loy perhaps, one that he could watch
over and over late into the night, charmed by lines
he'd buried long ago deep within his shallow heart.

TALKING DIRTY

Talking dirty's an art that love alone
won't allow us to perfect, though it can
provide opportunities for practice.

First you must learn that meaning does not count
(or counts for little).What matters instead
are the chewy fricatives, the liquids

washing against your teeth, the vowels stretched
to the breaking point, the sonic spillage
of arousal. Think, if you wish, in terms

of benedictions, formulae repeated
often and to many people. Dirty
words take on their power because they are

directed particularly to you,
even if there are others in earshot.
Oracular pronouncements, spells cast out

to unlock the mystery of our own
desires, they require a restraint at odds
with their blunt materials. Thus to get

the best effects—ones designed to bring down
the house—you must develop a keen sense
of timing, deploying with discretion

what is at best a highly circumscribed
vocabulary: silence as vital
as speech, what's not said equal to what is.

Love, for example, if mentioned at all,
must take on a different timbre, huskier
or more insidious, anything that

will distinguish it from normal usage.
Each syllable must bear its weight along
the tongue and back through the throat and deeper

from where the breath begins, resonating
through the whole body, even in whispers
so faint they are heard below consciousness

like a thought not yet risen to language,
an inside voice tingling across skin.
I've learned from experience volume

is not especially sexy, that words
spoken in the ear are better than those

proclaimed to the heavens, that it's better

to growl encouragement and coo commands
than the other way around, that you should
build up rhythms and then vary them,

syncopated to the thigh grown so taut
it might be plucked like a bass string.
Listen to the heaving of the breast. Match

word to action until air blows ragged
from your partner's rough lips or hones itself
to a knife-like sharpness that cuts right to

a catharsis that rattles down through your bones,
not with the usually pity and fear,
but with incomprehensible joy.

THE DISTRACTIONS OF BEAUTY

Right after my reading, he appeared
so I could sign his book and talk. He was
seventy-five or so, small and thin,
with a well-trimmed arc of snow-white beard.

His wife of nearly fifty years had died
a year before, he told me, and he'd been
faithful to her even to the end, but now,
now he felt he wanted to be gay.

He always knew that he was gay,
but somehow—times were different then—
he settled for a family and got
two sons, good boys, who now lived far away.

While he spoke, I noticed another man,
twenty-five I'd guess, who smiled at me,
then turned to show his bubble butt, the kind
that begs to be pricked so you can see just how

it would explode with pleasure. He told his sons
what he was up to, and one–the one who lived
in San Francisco–confessed that, like his dad,
he, too, was "a little gay," but later wed.

As for the other one … The bubble butt
clenched tight and then released his cheeks; they flexed
again and again like a pulsing sea anemone …
The brother? What of him? I made a vexed

attempt to retrieve my mind, which had gone adrift.
Well, he was much too busy to listen and put
the news away like an unwanted gift
he'd unwrap someday when he had time for it.

At last he said, "I must be boring you."
O those words stung! Callous and rude,
I'd been unbearably distracted
by an ass that had, alas, since left the room.

Forgive me. I should have known better
than let mere youth steer me blind,
for age must always go first, with beauty,
(if it comes at all) following close behind.

THE HITCHHIKER

My friends used to hitchhike cross country
with nothing more than a knapsack and a smile,
but I was far too chicken, even then,
of losing my way and ending up stuck
somewhere off the highway, hungry and sore,
the swollen nub of a sun going down fast
over a cornfield. Yet even the most
intrepid travelers stopped thumbing rides
sometime soon after the Summer of Love.
I can't tell what came first: the drivers afraid
of hitchhikers, their eyes aflame with acid,
or the hitchhikers afraid of the guys who'd stop
and leave them half-dead by the road with their pants
bunched around their ankles. Whatever the cause,
I haven't seen a hitchhiker in years,
though I look for them, for faces eager
and hopeful, young men standing at the ends
of off-ramps who might yet fulfill my dream:
picking up some kid in torn skintight jeans,
the sleeves of his T rolled up, his sun-streaked
hair caught in his lashes. As he leans
back in his seat, I can't help but notice
his excitement. I rest my hand gently
on his Levis, he spreads his legs further

apart. He's willing, oh more than willing,
to spend the night with me at the closest
motel as long as I drive him the next
morning no more than a half hour out
of my way to his folks. When we arrive
it's noon. Dad's pulling the first burgers off
the grill, his kid brother's in his baseball
uniform, and everyone's so happy
I've brought him home safe. I think of his ass
as they hug him, and the mole on his chest.
No, no, I have to be going. Well, yes,
I'll take a piece of rhubarb pie, and all
the way to the coast I can still smell him
fresh and clean and just-so-slightly acidic.

1968

For thirty years I've been trying to tell
this story, but I never get it right.
A week before we all are to go off
to college, my oldest friend and I drive
to Maine, just the two of us, to visit
Paul, a fellow classmate, who's summering
with his parents outside of Kennebunk.
On the last night we three are together,
Paul takes us to the breaker that stretches
its long arm into the harbor. I am
in love with Paul. It's the end of August.
The air has discovered again a chill
it had forgotten. The buoy bell rocks
gently in the water, and there are lights
far, far off that seem to have been scraped free
of any edges; they hover like breath
on a winter's day. Just a few feet out
on the breaker, the fog rolls in so thick
we cannot see each other. We grab hold
of the nearest hand so not to get lost
and fall unseen into the cold waters.
We inch our way along the long jetty,
and when we reach the end, the fog has cleared.
We can see out across the intricate

embroidery of waves to the clean stars.
We listen to the bells low like cattle
led to a meadow, and then we go back,
taking hands again through the wall of fog
until we've returned safe to shore. Early
the next morning, my friend and I drive home.
It is that simple. My life has never
been so simple again. That is why I
can never get it right, the telling, why
I must repeat it again and again
to myself as though I'm there now, as though
I were there still, as though I'd never turned
back again. This is the poem I can
never write. The poem I can never
stop writing because it is that simple.

ACKNOWLEDGMENTS

I want to thank the following journals and editors for allowing me to reprint poems: *Mary* for "In Nordstrom's," which also appeared in *Hot Sonnets,* edited by Clarinda Harriss and Moira Egan; *Bloom* for "A Valentine" and "The Embrace"; *The William & Mary Review* for "The Body Remembers"; *Ganymede* for the "Infinite Recession of the Object of Desire"; *The Kenyon Review* for "The Man Who Wasn't Loved Enough"; *Puerto del Sol* for "1968" and Lawrence Schimel who included "The Fortunate Light" in his anthology *Ells s'estimen: poems d'amour entre homes.*

Of course, I owe Lawrence Schimel thanks for suggesting this volume. I would also like to thank Daniel Mark Epstein who reads every poem I write and comments on them so thoughtfully. And John Lessner who has stood by me for more than a quarter of a century.

DAVID BERGMAN David Bergman (1950) is a poet and critic, educated at Kenyon College and The Johns Hopkins University, where he earned a Ph.D.

His previous poetry titles include *Heroic Measures* (Ohio State University Press) and *The Care and Treatment of Pain* (Kairos Editions) and he translated, with Katia Sainson, the *Selected Poems of Jean Sénac* (Sheep Meadow Press).

He is also the author of the critical works *The Violet Hour: The Violet Quill and the Making of Gay Culture* (Colombia University Press), *Camp Grounds: Style and Homosexuality* (The University of Massachussets Press) and *Gaiety Transfigured: Gay Self-Representation in American Literature* (The University of Wisconsin Press). In addition, he co-wrote, with Daniel Mark Epstien, *The Heath Guide to Literature* and *The Heath Guide to Poetry*.

He is the editor of important anthologies such as *The Violet Quill Reader: The Emergence of Gay Writing After Stonewall* (St. Martin's Press), *Gay American Autobiography: Writings from Whitman to Sedaris* (The University of Wisconsin Press), and three volumes of the *Men on Men* series (Penguin). In addition, he has edited critical collections of the writings of various writers, including John Ashbery and Edmund White.

He won the the George Elliston Poetry Prize for his poetry collection *Cracking the Code* and the Lambda Literary Award for his anthology *Men on Men* 2000.

He is the poetry editor of *Gay and Lesbian Review Worldwide* and Professor of English & Cultural Studies at Towson University in Maryland. He lives in Baltimore with his partner of many years, John Lessner.

A MIDSUMMER NIGHT'S PRESS was founded by
Lawrence Schimel in New Haven, CT in 1991. Using a
letterpress, it published broadsides of poems by
Nancy Willard, Joe Haldeman, and Jane Yolen, among
others, in signed, limited editions of 126 copies,
numbered 1-100 and lettered A-Z. One of the
broadsides —"Will" by Jane Yolen—won a Rhysling
Award. In 1993, the publisher moved to New York and
the press went on hiatus until 2007, when it began
publishing perfect-bound, commercially-printed
books, primarily under two imprints:

FABULA RASA: devoted to works inspired by
mythology, folklore, and fairy tales. Titles from this
imprint include *Fairy Tales for Writers* by Lawrence
Schimel, *Fortune's Lover: A Book of Tarot Poems* by
Rachel Pollack, *Fairy Tales in Electri-city* by Francesca
Lia Block, *The Last Selchie Child* by Jane Yolen, and
What If What's Imagined Were All True by Roz Kaveney.

BODY LANGUAGE: devoted to texts exploring questions
of gender and sexual identity. Titles from this imprint
include *This is What Happened in Our Other Life* by
Achy Obejas; *Banalities* by Brane Mozetic, translated
from the Slovene by Elizabeta Zargi with Timothy Liu;
Handmade Love by Julie R. Enszer; *Mute* by Raymond
Luczak; *Milk and Honey: A Celebration of Jewish
Lesbian Poetry* edited by Julie R. Enszer; *Dialectic of
the Flesh* by Roz Kaveney; and *Deleted Names* by
Lawrence Schimel.